# How to Start and Sustain a Faith-Based MEN'S GROUP

# How to Start and Sustain a Faith-Based MEN'S GROUP

John D. Schroeder

ABINGDON PRESS / NASHVILLE

HOW TO START AND SUSTAIN A
FAITH-BASED MEN'S GROUP

*Copyright © 2003 by Abingdon Press*

*This book is printed on acid-free, elemental-chlorine–free paper.*

**Library of Congress Cataloging-in-Publication Data**

Schroeder, John D.
    How to start and sustain a faith-based men's group / John D.
Schroeder.
        p. cm.
    ISBN 0-687-07378-2 (alk. paper)
    1. Church group work with men. I. Title.

    BV4440.S37 2003
    239'.081—dc21

                            2003012958

03 04 05 06 07 08 09 10 11 12—10 9 8 7 6 5 4 3 2 1
MANUFACTURED IN THE UNITED STATES OF AMERICA

# CONTENTS

# INTRODUCTION

When the wealthy eccentric William Beckford decided to build his dream home in 1794, it was the beginning of one of the biggest and most extravagant follies in British construction history.

Beckford's great ambition was to build a huge Gothic "abbey" on his estate, complete with lofty halls and high towers. He began construction of his home by erecting a wall around his entire estate to prevent others from viewing his project. He then brought in hundreds of men to work around the clock on his future home.

When work did not go fast enough, Beckford took over supervision of the project himself. As an incentive to finish on time, Beckford rewarded daily accomplishment with larger and larger rations of liquor. Eventually his workers became drunk and incompetent.

But Beckford's biggest mistake, as well as the literal downfall of the entire project, was his impatience. Always in a hurry, Beckford saw no need for a proper foundation to be dug. His workers built the huge structure on a foundation originally meant for a small summer home. At Christmastime, the abbey's kitchen was able to be used to cook Christmas dinner, but its walls collapsed later that day. The main tower fell six years later. Gradually, the remaining buildings fell as well. Today there is not much left of Fonthill Abbey, the impractical fantasy of William Beckford.

The importance of a firm foundation is just as vital today, not only in buildings but also in constructing new programs within the Christian church. Many familiar hymns remind us to build our lives, our programs, and our congregations on the rock of Christ. A faith-based foundation is needed for long-lasting results. Christ needs to be the architect of all our dreams.

To build a men's group takes faith and a partnership with God. It is an opportunity to change lives within and outside your congregation. It takes time, patience, prayer, and people working together in order to construct programs that benefit men and their families. It is an exciting opportunity because as you begin, you have no idea what great accomplishments will result from everyone's efforts.

It is not something you do alone. God partici-
pates. Each man in the group plays an important
role in the destination of the group. You work as a
team to achieve God's will and the objectives you
set forth. And it's not always easy, but it certainly
can be rewarding for all involved.

Your planning begins by looking at needs. Talk to
men, and listen. You will hear a variety of needs,
ranging from spiritual concerns, to building relationships with others, to a desire to give back to the
church or community. These needs will be
expressed in different ways. Some of what you hear
may surprise you. Your original idea may take an
entirely different direction. That's why it is so important to listen and discover what's on the minds of the
men in your congregation and community.

It is also important to remember that all groups
are unique. No two in the world are exactly alike
because each one consists of unique individuals.
The conversations and activities in your group will
be different from those in men's groups in other
congregations. The size of the group may be small
or it may number in the hundreds. Some groups
gather monthly, while others gather weekly. There
are so many variables that in the end your men's
group will certainly be one of a kind.

And because each group and individual is unique,
acceptance is crucial to this ministry. All men who

participate in the group must be accepted just as they are. Each will be at a different point on his spiritual journey. Some will believe that Jesus Christ is their Lord and Savior. Others may be nonbelievers. Many may consider themselves seekers, or believers in "something." Each one, however, will have something important to contribute to the group.

As you begin, take a lesson from William Beckford, and learn from his mistakes. Build a proper foundation. Be patient. Set realistic goals and do some planning. Listen to others and work as a team in constructing your vision.

Finally, since this group will be based on the faith of all participants, use the power of prayer to guide you and your group toward the destination God has in mind for you. The journey will be one like you have never had before, and God will be with you every step of the way.

# CHAPTER 1

# Initial Decisions
and Planning

Where to begin? That's the question as you consider the many aspects of starting and sustaining a faith-based men's group. There are people to see, places to go, and things to do. And the good news is that everything will get done as you take things one step at a time.

Accomplishment begins with planning and establishing priorities for what you hope will be a successful and valuable new ministry within your congregation. You need to look at the big picture, always focusing on the needs of group participants. There are many opportunities for men's ministries in the church.

Initially you may have thought of starting a men's small-group Bible study that meets weekly. That's a great idea. But what other options are available? Perhaps there is a need to strengthen father and son relationships within the congregation, so some father and son activities might be in order. Retreats are another possibility. Or maybe the men in your church are interested in mission and would like to focus on it through weekly meetings. Add to that, community and church service projects and throw in a men's church softball or basketball team. Now you are seeing a greater ministry potential.

Keep all of these options in mind as you begin your planning. Ideas for programs and activities will be covered later in this book. For now, take the first step by examining your objectives.

## ✧ Objectives

Why do you want to start (and sustain) a faith-based men's group? What do you hope to accomplish? These two questions are critical as you begin the process of turning your dream into reality. Let's take the first question.

Your desire to begin a ministry for men needs to be put in writing. You want to start a group because (1) you see a need, (2) it will strengthen your church, and/or (3) there are service projects to be accomplished. There are many other reasons. Put these reasons down on paper. Think about them. Pray about them. This is your first step.

As you think about needs, remember that people join groups in order to have their own needs met.

The men who attend your gatherings come for a reason and with an agenda. One man may come to make new friends, while another may attend for spiritual growth. A men's group can satisfy multiple needs, but it helps if these needs are considered in initial planning.

A second step is to consider what you hope to accomplish. Let's say for example that your desire is to start a weekly small group for men. If that would be the case, what objectives would you have for the group? List some outcomes, goals, or objectives of any activity you may be considering. If you put these objectives together in the form of a mission statement, you have the beginning of a solid foundation on which to build the group.

Once you have your mission statement, share it with others. Refine it. Be open to other objectives and ideas from other men. A mission statement is not set in concrete. It can change and evolve as your men's group develops. While its purpose is to focus on objectives, a mission statement is more than that. It also serves as a summary of what your group is all about. It conveys information to others. A mission statement can promote your group. William Beckford's mission was to build an impressive mansion as fast as possible. Your mission statement should be detailed and comprehensive, considering all aspects of your vision. The greater thought that is put into your vision, the better the results.

## ✧ Men's Issues

As previously mentioned, men's issues are an important consideration in your initial planning. What needs do men have? What issues do most men share? What needs are strong enough to bring men together in a group within your congregation?

Men may share an interest in sports, politics, the environment, crime prevention, automobiles, and dozens of other topics, but this is not necessarily the basis for a faith-based men's group. You are looking for needs and issues that fit within a ministry.

One way to begin a needs assessment is to talk to the men within your congregation. You might create a list of needs and then share it with some men you know. Ask if there is anything missing from the list. Remember that you are looking for needs that can be met through the ministry of a faith-based men's group. Here are some ideas.

Men have a need for strong relationships with others. There is the need for friendship with other men. Married men desire a better relationship with their spouses. Parents want to improve their relationships with children. Single men may have a multitude of relationship questions regarding dating.

Some men may be working at strengthening relationships with their own parents or perhaps with their in-laws. These relationship issues can be tackled from a Christian perspective within a small group at your church. Men can share their thoughts and experiences with others concerning relationships.

Men have a need for spiritual nourishment. Men want to have a stronger relationship with God. They may want to learn about prayer, or become better at reading the Bible. Married men want to know how to maintain a strong Christian family. Others may be interested in mission and how to introduce Jesus to friends or coworkers. Men can help other men strengthen their faith within a small-group setting.

Men have a need for advice from other men on how to tackle the tough issues of life. They want to know how to live as Christian men in a world of joblessness, crime, divorce, addictions, illness, accidents, and death of friends, family, or parents. Men want to live with integrity, compassion, honesty, and a positive attitude. They want to know how to confront daily challenges and deal with them. A Bible study or one of many Christian books would be appropriate to meet these needs within a small-group setting.

Men have a need to be physically fit. It is often quite difficult for men to get the exercise they need.

Being overweight is a national epidemic. The answer could be regular physical activities such as golf, basketball, volleyball, softball, running, or walking. Whether it is competitive or just for fun, sports are an excellent way to bring men together to keep in shape and to gain new Christian friends at the same time.

Men have a need to contribute within the church. Many men want to go beyond Sunday worship and work with other men in maintaining or serving the congregation. It might be as simple as compiling a list of men interested in caring for the church grounds and property. Another ministry could be a men's chorus. Men can be Sunday school and confirmation teachers. They can also be mentors. The men of your church could form a ministry of a service corps to meet these and other needs.

Men have a need to contribute to the community. Look at the needs of your community and determine how the men of your church can best meet those needs. This team ministry could include crime patrols, raising funds for people in need, securing transitional housing, building a playground, or any number of needed projects.

These are just some of the needs that can be met through a faith-based men's group within your congregation. Open your eyes and ears to all of the opportunities around you for men's ministries.

## ✧ Ages and Interests

Chances are the participants of your faith-based men's group will be of different ages and have different interests, which will need to be taken into consideration. Here are some of the different general categories of men and their related interests.

High school and college men offer youthful insight into a men's group. Their world often will revolve around education and dating relationships. They are just starting out in life and are still finding themselves. They may have part-time jobs or be looking for work. Lack of money may be a concern for them. Some may be dealing with issues including independence, identity, and intimacy. Young men can greatly benefit from life experiences of those who are older. Mature Christian men can help provide a strong spiritual foundation for those who are younger.

Single men who are out of college and just entering the work force may have similar interests and issues of college men. They may also be on their own for the first time. Christian issues related to dating and relationships may be of interest to them. They will welcome advice and support from older men who can share their life experiences.

Married men with or without children can add a valuable perspective to a faith-based men's group. Between work and family life, one of their major issues may be just finding time to get everything done. They want success at work and at home, but they also have spiritual needs to be met. Married men may be interested in relationship advice and friendships with other Christian men.

Retired men often have the available time and the life experience to share, which makes them welcome additions to men's groups. These men can share their faith journey and help those who seek spiritual direction. Some retired men have health issues and welcome the support and encouragement of younger men.

Non-Christian men may find their way to your faith-based men's group through one of your members or just on their own. They may consider themselves to be seekers. These men may want spiritual information or answers that Christian men can provide. Like all others, they need to be accepted and welcomed into the group.

You need to be aware of the benefits of diversity through men who do not represent the majority of your group. These may include men of a different race or ethnic background, gay men, immigrants, or persons with disabilities. They may share a different perspective on the world that is valuable for a small group. They need to be accepted as they are and encouraged on their spiritual journey.

Chances are your faith-based men's group will include many of these men from these broad general categories. They may have different interests and backgrounds, but God has brought them together for spiritual growth and Christian friendship. Once your group is underway, differences may fade, and the group will discover the many things they all have in common.

## ✧ Decisions and Research

Once you have some idea about why you want to form a men's group and have put together an initial mission statement, it is time to make some decisions about your prospective participants. One decision is around the number of participants that you anticipate.

If you are planning to begin with a small-group Bible study, the decision process is somewhat simple. If, however, you are planning multiple small groups, along with retreats, father-son events, and other programming, it gets a bit more complicated. You'll first want to look at the amount of space available. Are you planning to have your gatherings in a large room or small room? Do you need a gymnasium, or can you hold some activities outdoors? Will you be meeting on Sunday mornings, and if so, will there be space available? Or are you looking at a weekday evening?

You may want the group to be small enough so that everyone gets a chance to participate, especially if you are considering starting a Bible study or small group. One option is to break down the large group into several small groups for some events. Remember that some men will be absent from time to time. Think about seating, comfort, and the ability to hear one another.

Will your group be open to men of all ages? Will they belong to your church, or do you hope to attract men from the community? These questions could be answered within your mission statement.

The next step in the creation of your group should be some research that can increase the chances of your success in launching the group. Create a list of potential members and conduct some research interviews. Get to know your potential group members. Meet them face-to-face. Learn about their situations, their needs, and their interests. This is your opportunity to become an "expert" on the needs of men within your congregation and/or community.

Your survey should gauge their interest in participating in a men's group. What would they like the group to do? Give them some possible activities as examples. Would they be willing to attend on

Sunday mornings during the Sunday school hour? Would they prefer Saturday morning? What time is best? You might also ask them if they have a friend or neighbor who might be interested.

Interview as many men as possible, then sit down and review your findings. Learn from what you were told. Be flexible. What you heard from them may be different from your original vision. Continue to build a solid foundation for your group, and eventually everything will fall into place.

### ✧ Leadership Decisions

Now you are ready to focus on the question of leadership. You have several options open to you, including having a single leader or a leadership team. Consider the qualities you will be looking for in a leader.

You will want a man who relates well to others. One of the most important traits for a leader is to be a good listener. You will want someone who can invest the time to launch a program and do what is necessary to keep it running. If the group will meet weekly, the leader's schedule must be free so he can be at the meeting each week.

Another quality needed in a leader is creativity. Is this person able to conceive and sustain activities that will keep men interested? A leader also needs a strong organizational ability. This is the ability to handle or delegate a multitude of tasks, making sure all the details get covered. You also want a leader who can be counted on to do the work, while at the same time being responsive to the needs of the group.

Beyond the tasks involved in starting a group, a leader often acts as the facilitator of each meeting. The leader keeps track of individual members. Small-group members let him know if they are unable to attend a meeting. The leader is responsible for notifying participants if the meeting or event is canceled. Some responsibilities of the leader certainly can be delegated.

The leader is the shepherd of the group, looking out for the flock. If problems develop within the group, he deals with them. If a small-group discussion is offered, lesson preparation is involved each week, as well as for any postdiscussion, group activities, or social events.

Taking all of the above into consideration, the question becomes, can one person possess all of these traits and fulfill all of these roles, or is a leadership team required? Here are a few options to consider:

- The leader could be a church pastor or a retired pastor.
- The leader could be a seminary student, working for part-time pay or as part of an internship.

- The leader could be a member of the congregation who has the time and interest in leading a group.

Another option is a leadership team that makes decisions together and delegates responsibilities. If you are responsible for establishing a leadership team, recruit carefully. Do not simply ask for volunteers. You could end up with a group of men who lack the combination of skills required to meet the demands of operating a men's group.

## ✧ Costs and Funding

It doesn't take much money to start a men's group. Typical costs might include a text for small-group discussions, costs for promoting the group, snacks, and supplies for activities. An additional expense would be incurred if the leader is being paid for his time.

The cost of materials, such as a text for group discussions, might be covered by each of the participants. Refreshments could be a shared group expense. The cost of other items might be provided in the church budget, or perhaps someone in the congregation could donate funds. Another alternative would be to seek donations from local businesses. For example, a business might sponsor your softball or basketball team.

# CHAPTER 2

# Activities and Options

Once you have a proper foundation for your faith-based men's group, consider what type of activities and groups to offer the men of your church. By this time, you should have some idea about what programming is both needed and desired. The feedback from the men of your church should be closely considered as you begin this planning.

There is a full range of options available to you in men's ministry. These options include a weekly one-hour informal discussion group, a number of small groups, Bible studies, recreational activities, social events, special events, athletic events, and retreats. You can offer as little or as much as you want. You may want to start small and increase the amount of programming with time.

Your programming will be determined by your number of participants, available space in your facility, the interests of the men, and how much time the leader has to invest in this ministry. The needs of the participants will be a primary factor in your decisions.

Programming may seek to meet the spiritual, social, or recreational needs of your participants, but not necessarily all three. A faith-based men's group usually will focus on the spiritual; however, social needs will be met to some extent with any kind of programming. You can also be experimental in your programming, keeping what works and changing what doesn't. There may be a period of trial and error for up to a year before you find programs that meet needs while generating attendance.

## ✧ Quality Programs

It is the men of your church who will determine how well your programming is received. They are the judge and jury. If they do not find a gathering worthy of their time, they will not come back. Quality is essential. When starting out, it is vital to be organized, to have the necessary program materials in place, and to offer a welcoming atmosphere.

In your planning, consider the many activities against which your men's group competes. For married men, family demands will often vie for their time and attention. Younger, single men may have to decide between church or their girlfriend, at times. And sometimes after a long, hard day at work, resting and relaxing at home will have strong appeal. When you program activities at church, you are in a battle to win a man's free time.

Attending an event at church usually will be cheaper than going to a movie or to dinner; money does matter. The church is also a good refuge from family or work troubles. Men know they can get advice and support from friends at church. Christian fellowship is a definite drawing card. Also, remember that the weather can either hurt or help attendance.

In the end, however, the question remains, what would cause the men you hope to attract to choose your men's group instead of some other activity?

A group that makes a man feel welcome and among friends always has an edge in the competition. Add to that quality programming, and you are off to a good start. That is why preparation pays huge dividends. The more you prepare, the easier it will be to get your group off the ground. It always is evident to others when you have done your homework and have your act together.

If you are leading a session, prepare well in advance. Have adequate copies of materials available. If you are unsure how to carry out an activity, first try it out with family members or friends.

Think *quality* when it comes to your meeting room. Some men may be brand new to the congregation. Look at your meeting room as if you were seeing it for the first time. What is your first impression? What can you change to make it more inviting? How can a stranger coming into the church for the first time know that a men's group meets in "Room 102"? If you want men who are parents to come, child care is another issue. Will you offer a supervised room for their children, or do the parents need to make their own arrangements?

If a leader of a men's group should cultivate any one virtue, it is hospitality. Create a safe place to talk with other men. Make it a friendly place that welcomes all men, including men without connections to your church. Offer an oasis in the midst of a shifting, uncertain life. Provide more than you promise.

If you are the leader, think of those who attend your programs as if they were guests in your home. Consider what you can do to make them feel more comfortable. How can you welcome them? How can you help the men to feel that they belong here? How might you refresh them? And most important, how can you be sure that when they leave, they will be looking forward to the time they can return?

### ✧ Small Groups

Many congregations offer small-group discussions or Bible studies to meet the spiritual needs of men. These might take place on Sunday morning between worship services, on Saturday morning, or on a weekday evening in conjunction with other church activities such as choir practice or fellowship meals. Chances are you have participated in or perhaps led a small-group discussion in the past. Here are some of the basics:

People helping people grow in faith is the ministry of the small group. A small group is usually a group of twelve or fewer who gather together to study God's Word and encourage one another in faith. Just as Jesus used his twelve disciples to change the world, God uses small groups to change lives.

Small groups are an opportunity for individuals to discuss issues of faith in a nonthreatening and supportive environment. It is a place where the men in your group will learn from other men. It is a place where you can safely ask questions. In small groups, members share ideas and experiences.

In preparing to launch your small group, you will need to consider a number of aspects about meetings. In most cases, the number of times your small group will meet will be decided by your choice of topic and material. For instance, if the book you select for study has twelve chapters, then most likely you would meet for twelve weeks then continue on with another book, with or without a break between them.

Another idea is to have an "open" small group with a different topic each time, using the Bible as the text. The leader would create a topic and discussion questions. Anyone could show up and join the discussion. There would be no participant preparation needed, nor any strict attendance requirements. Men would attend as they are able. For example, it could be publicized that your church has a faith-based men's group that meets each Tuesday night at 7:00 for ninety minutes, and all are welcome.

The traditional alternative is to have a small group that meets weekly for a set number of weeks (for example, as determined by the number of chapters in your study material), with the same participants each week. Each member would have his own copy of the study text, read the lesson for each week, and come prepared to discuss it. This format does make it difficult to add new participants several weeks into the discussion. It also obligates the members to make a commitment to attend each week in order to have enough people for a lively discussion.

The length of each session for many small groups is from one hour to ninety minutes. You want to allow enough time for social time, topic discussion, and perhaps an activity. This would be in addition to any time spent for a large group activity or recreational activity. Most participants find they can spare an hour a week, plus travel time to and from the discussion location. You want to allow enough time to complete your small-group discussion while respecting individual time restrictions.

It is important to note that perhaps all the men in your group will want to attend the small-group discussion, but may be interested in the activity that comes before or after the discussion. Some men's groups may offer basketball or volleyball in a gym or outdoors either before or after the discussion. Flexible scheduling helps you meet the needs and interests of your participants.

## ✧ Discussion Materials

When it comes to discussion material for your small group, there are thousands of options. You may already know the text you want to use, and if so, you can move on to other decisions.

If you are undecided, two options include using a Christian-themed book or the Bible for your discussion. Your local Christian bookstore or church library may provide ideas and options. You can also use the Internet to search for potential discussion material.

Here are some starters using Christian themes:

> The basics of Christianity
> Learning your identity as a Christian
> Gaining spiritual maturity
> Living as a Christian
> The power of the Lord's Prayer
> Living a life of faith in a secular world
> Learning about Christ's twelve apostles

There are also many secular topics that tackle men's issues from a Christian perspective:

- Fatherhood—what it means to be a Christian father
- Forgiveness in relationships
- Expressing anger
- Coping with change
- Male depression
- The dynamics of grief
- Creating spiritual relationships
- Issues relating to divorce
- Domestic violence
- Helping boys become Christian men
- Male power
- Retirement issues
- Christian dating

If you are planning a small-group study, there are a few things to keep in mind. You may want to encourage all participants to use the same version of the Bible. If this is the case, the leader should determine the version, perhaps with input from participants. You could ask what version each participant owns and go with the majority. Another idea is for the leader to have several versions on hand during the meeting to check different translations.

Your local bookstore is an excellent source for locating discussion guides for various books of the

Bible. Discussion guides contain questions for the group to answer, and they sometimes include group activities. Your first step is to select which book of the Bible you want to study. You will want to select a guide that is compatible with your beliefs and your denomination. Look at how many weeks or sessions the guide is divided into and compare the costs of various guides. You also need to decide if you want to purchase just one study guide for the leader, or if you want each member to have a guide and access to the weekly questions. Your pastor may also have suggestions on which study guide to use.

If you want to use a Christian-themed book, there are many to choose from. Your church library and local Christian bookstore are great places to begin your search. Also, ask the men in your congregation for suggestions. Many Christian publishers, such as Abingdon Press, are now including study guides in the backs of books. Separate companion study guides for Christian books are also available from many publishers. Many books are located in the inspirational or Christian Living sections of bookstores.

Not all books come with a study guide containing questions for group discussion. Having a ready-made study guide makes it easier for the discussion leader, but you can lead a discussion without one. In such a case, the leader and/or participants would be responsible for coming up with questions.

Another option is to study a secular book and focus on how it relates to your Christian faith. For example, a book on job hunting could be used for a small group if many of the men in your congregation are unemployed or looking for new jobs. Topics for each session could include prayer, networking, contacts within the church, Internet searches, trust in God, and other related themes.

Take care in selecting a book. Your choice can affect the quality of the discussions. You want to look for a subject that will hold the interest of your small group for the duration of the class. You may want to read the book in its entirety first to determine if you can live with it for several months.

Consider if the text would encourage good discussion. Is it suited for men? Does it contain stories that illustrate Christian themes? Is it easy to read? Finally, ask yourself if this is a book that is worth the time that will be invested. Consider whether your participants will gain spiritual growth as a result of reading this book. You might want to take one or more members of your men's group along when you look at books. Consider their opinions on topics and books.

Remember that the book you select is a catalyst for God to work within your group. Much of the spiritual growth may come from the discussions and from members ministering to one another.

## ✧ Recreational Options

Physical fitness is important for many men, and what better place than church to exercise alongside other Christian men? You can build your programming so that it includes a recreational activity before or after the small-group session. Another option is to have a monthly recreational game or event.

Recreational activities are often included in programming to offer variety. While a Bible study may not appeal to all men, an occasional basketball or volleyball game might generate attendance. Sometimes men come for the recreation and then decide to stay for the small group. Some athletic activity is also very appealing to those who sit at a desk all day at work.

If a number of men in your congregation are overweight, consider the combination of a health-issues small group followed by a physical activity. Members could discuss their progress each week and be encouraged by other men. Your faith-based wellness group could utilize the Bible or a Christian-themed book to talk about health issues.

If your church has a gymnasium, you have an advantage when it comes to recreational programming. Activities such as men's basketball or volleyball can be scheduled on a regular basis. If your church does not have a gym, check with neighboring churches and schools.

Some recreational options for your men's group include golf, volleyball, bowling, softball, basketball, swimming, running, hiking, soccer, flag football, and tennis. Most of these sports require equipment that could be obtained from members of the group, from church members, or from a sponsoring local business. If your church has a gym, chances are they also have equipment for gym sports.

A number of these activities are outdoor sports that can be played in a nearby park during warm months. Volleyball and basketball can move into a gym during the winter. Most sports are inexpensive, which is another plus for participants.

If you do offer a recreational event, check with your church about their liability insurance coverage.

## ✧ Father-Son Events

Your men's group ministry can help bring fathers and sons closer together by planning and scheduling some programming that includes them both. Dads often wish they could spend more time with their sons, while boys can spend time with friends and/or make new friends during these events.

It doesn't have to be anything elaborate. It could be as simple as hosting a father-son board game night in your fellowship hall. Each dad could bring a family board game and snacks to share. You could switch games and players during the evening to facilitate the guys getting to know one another.

Another father-son event could be a church-sponsored afternoon or evening at a local sporting event. Whether it is watching a baseball, basketball, or hockey game, it's spending time together that counts. The guys could meet in the church parking lot and carpool to the game. Afterwards, they could go out for pizza.

Use your creativity to come up with ways to bring fathers and sons closer together within a Christian atmosphere. Father-son retreats are a great way guys can spend quality time together. Ask the members of your group what activities they enjoy with their sons. You'll receive some great ideas on how to program for fathers and sons.

## ✧ Retreats

Some men's groups offer seasonal retreats. A retreat presents an excellent opportunity for group members to strengthen their bonds of friendship and grow spiritually. Usually the retreat runs from Friday night to Sunday afternoon. Locations can include the cabin of a group member, a church camp, a state park, a ski lodge, or a beachside setting.

The leader or leadership team can select the location and plan the activities. The retreat can have a theme, if you desire. Transportation can be by church bus or van, or by carpool, with drivers being reimbursed for gas. Activities can include a mix of spiritual, recreational, and social events. Meals and snacks need to be well planned in advance.

The cost per person is determined by the leader or planning committee once all costs have been considered. Asking for a commitment and a deposit weeks in advance is wise. Set a firm deadline for registrations. Some churches offer scholarships for retreats for persons with low income.

Encourage the men to take along their cameras and to take lots of photographs. After the retreat, create a photo display at church so all church members can become better acquainted with the group. The display can also serve as a way of attracting more members.

## ✧ Service Projects

The men of your group can perform service projects or fund-raisers as a way of contributing to the church or to the community. This is a great way to put the talents and skills of the men to work and to build bonds of friendship and teamwork as they work together toward a single goal. In return, the men receive appreciation and knowledge that they made a difference by giving of their time.

Service projects and fund-raisers can be conducted any time of year. All that is required is a commitment from group members to give of their time and talent. Ideas for projects can come from the leader, group members, the church pastor, or others. There are multiple needs within every church and community, so it should not be difficult to find a project that matches the abilities of the group.

A common community service project is to paint the interior or exterior of an older adult's home. Often the recipient will furnish the paint and food in exchange for the painting. Raking leaves in the fall and doing yard work are also appreciated services. Men can give of their time by serving as mentors within the community. Men who are handy with tools can perform household repairs or car repairs for local citizens who are in need but cannot afford to pay for those services. Take a skills survey of those in your group, and you'll be surprised at what your group is equipped to do.

The men in your group can also serve your church. Your faith-based men's group could function as a service corps and perform needed tasks with the church, such as repairs and landscaping. Computer skills are valuable within any congregation. If some of the men are blessed with great voices or musical talent, they could contribute at worship occasionally as a men's singing group or perform in the church talent show. Men can also be mentors to boys within the church who don't have fathers. The men of your group could teach Sunday school together, work the sound system, serve as ushers, or perform any number of needed tasks. As the leader of a men's group, you have the opportunity to help put talent to work.

If your men's group plays sports, you could have a sports-related fund-raiser for the church or local charities. The men could solicit pledges from family, friends, and church members. Often local businesses will sponsor the event and provide pizza and soft drinks.

### ✧ Special Events

Some men's groups offer a monthly social event where members can become better acquainted and deepen their friendships. These events can be scheduled, planned, and implemented by the leader or by volunteers within the group. The scheduled event should be announced weeks in advance so that everyone knows about it. Some groups schedule a social event for a certain day each month, such as every third Saturday, so members can put it on their calendars.

The best part about having a social event is that it can be as simple or as elaborate as you wish. The cost usually is minimal, and some events require no cost. You can be as creative as you want. And with a variety of options available, the men in your group need never be bored with the same old thing.

Some popular options:

- See movies—go to the local movie theater as a group.
- Play cards—get a few decks of cards and have some fun.
- Fishing—a great Saturday morning group activity.
- Go out to eat—everyone likes food!
- Take in a sports event—see a collegiate or professional game together.
- Play miniature golf together—cheap fun. Compete for the lowest score!

These are just a few of the things you can do as a group that will help everyone get to know one another better. Some of your events may require a carpool, while others can take place at church. Ask the men for suggestions on what they want to do.

# CHAPTER 3

# The First Meeting

It's time to bring the men together for the first meeting! Once you have decided on programming options and when to offer them, you are ready to begin your faith-based men's group. Your next step is to publicize your men's group and to prepare for that important first meeting.

Set a goal of how many men you want to attend. If you are having just one small group, you probably want only six to twelve men to accept your invitation. If you can handle two small groups, double that number. If you plan to launch your group with a men's basketball or volleyball game, you'll know how many players you need or can accommodate. You also could begin your faith-based men's group ministry by going fishing or by attending a sports event together. If you have an event planned that can accommodate any number of people who show up, go for it! Select whatever activity will start your group out on the right step. Your goal is to get men together and get them talking.

Try to get a firm commitment from those you invite to attend this first meeting. Personal invitations are the best way to generate attendance. Flyers in the church bulletin can be ignored, but a personal invitation almost always gets an answer. Use your entire list of prospects. Make recruitment personal. Telephone them. Email them. Get some carpools started. Again, keep track of how many men plan on attending.

Publicize the start of your men's group in whatever media might be available. Announce it at worship. Talk to as many as you can when worship services are over. Get it in the church bulletin and monthly newsletter. You have two goals: for men to read about the group and be given a personal invitation.

Encourage those you invite to bring a friend along. This can provide the double benefit of increasing attendance, as well as making those who attend more comfortable because they will know at least one person there. But keep track of the total number of men planning to attend or bring a friend if the size of your group needs to be limited.

You might want to phone or email each person prior to the meeting with a reminder of the starting time and location. A telephone call provides the opportunity to get to know persons a bit better, and you can answer any questions they have.

## ✧ Tips and Ideas

This section is intended to guide you through your first session. You may be both excited and nervous the day or evening of your initial meeting. You are about to begin a valuable ministry that can change men's lives. Share with God in prayer your feelings, and ask for guidance as you get ready to lead your first session.

Before you begin, remember that this meeting probably will serve just two purposes. First, people will have time to get to know one another. Second, it will be a time for you to provide basic information to them and answer any questions. If you are starting a small group, there may not be enough time for discussion of the first lesson. You could use the time to hand out a copy of the book you will be using and give an overview.

Remember the importance of making a good first impression. Make the first session festive. Have fun. Provide a balance of fellowship and information-giving. It's best to arrive early at the location of your first meeting so you can welcome all the participants and make introductions. Chances are you and your participants may not know everyone there. Try some icebreakers to get the men to socialize.

Some icebreaker ideas:

- Give each man a sheet of paper and a pen as he enters. Ask them to get the autographs of all the other men.
- Have each person share his favorite place, favorite person, and favorite pastime, recreation, or hobby. Since the first person sets the tone, select someone who feels comfortable sharing with others. Encourage the men to say as little or as much as they feel comfortable sharing with the group.
- Break the group into pairs and have each man interview his partner for five minutes. Information such as name, family background, occupation, and hobbies may be shared. After the interviews are completed, each man introduces his new friend to the rest of the group.
- Ask participants to mingle and discover a common bond with each of the other men. It may be wearing the same color shoes, being born in the same city or town, or having graduated from the same high school. Have them report their common bonds to the group.

Use your own imagination to think up other ways to get the guys talking to one another. You may want to have an icebreaker at the start of both the first and second sessions. Depending on the size of your group, you may want to give each man a name tag for this first meeting.

After the icebreaker, get the group seated. Start on time. Welcome them. Share your enthusiasm for this opportunity. If you are going to study a book, introduce it. You may want to cover why this book was selected and give an overview. Also, discuss what you want to accomplish as a faith-based men's group. Share the group's mission statement. Ask the men to briefly talk about why they decided to attend and what they expect to receive and learn.

Review the format of future meetings and tell how much time will be spent on each segment. If you are having a small group, here is an example:

1. Social time
2. Check-in, where each person reports how he is, what's new since last week, and so forth
3. Announcements by the leader
4. Book discussion (which can be followed by a group activity)
5. Closing prayer
6. Refreshments, social time

If you have planned to begin book discussion with your first meeting, go ahead. Following are some suggestions for the leader on how to facilitate the discussion.

## ✧ Leader Guidelines

1. Know your people. Good teachers know that they teach persons, not lessons.

2. Avoid controlling the group. One of the most common mistakes a leader makes is to try to control what happens in the group. The group as a whole is responsible for what takes place during the session itself.

3. Keep aware of what is going on in the group. How are the men responding and interacting? Is discussion lagging due to lack of interest? Do you need to allow more time for an activity that is going well? You want to remain flexible.

4. If your group is studying a book, then prior to the meeting, read the chapter and highlight important sentences or paragraphs. Make notes in the margins if you desire. Get comfortable with the material.

5. If your book contains questions or comes with a study guide that contains questions, review them in advance. Remember, you don't have to use all the questions in the study guide, and you can create your own.

6. If your book does not contain discussion questions, you can write your own. Jot down questions as they come to you while reading the lesson. You may want to begin group discussion each week with a general question such as, What new insights did you receive from reading this chapter? You also can

ask group members to begin the discussion with their own questions or a topic they want to discuss. (All of the questions do not have to come from you.) You can write questions about the meanings of words. Ask members to talk about a personal experience with the topic of the session. One way to conclude discussion is by asking a general question such as, How has this lesson or this discussion helped or challenged you? Try to prepare about a dozen questions for each chapter.

7. For the first couple of sessions, you may begin by reminding the men that not everyone may feel comfortable reading aloud, answering questions, or participating in group activities. Encourage them to participate as they feel comfortable doing so.

8. You could begin discussion by reviewing the main points of the chapter and providing the group with a summary. You may ask the men what they saw as highlights.

9. Encourage questions. Remind the group that all questions are valid as part of the learning process. When you ask questions, you give permission for people to talk to others, exchanging thoughts and feelings.

10. Even if some men don't talk during a discussion, you can be assured there is an internal dialogue enabling them to get in touch with their thoughts and feelings.

11. Some questions may be more difficult to answer than others. If you ask a question and no one responds, begin the discussion by venturing an answer yourself. Then ask for comments and other answers. Remember that some questions may have multiple answers.

12. Ask the questions "Why?" or "Why do you believe that?" to help continue a discussion and give it greater depth.

13. Give everyone a chance to talk. Keep the conversation moving. Occasionally you may want to direct a question to a specific person who has been quiet. "Do you have anything to add?" is a good follow-up question to another person. If the conversation gets off track, move ahead by asking the next question.

14. Before moving from questions to activities, ask the men if they have any questions that have not been answered.

15. Remember that as a leader, you do not have to know all the answers. Some answers may come from group members. Other answers may even need a bit of research. Your job is to keep the discussion moving and to encourage participation.

16. Be grateful and supportive. Thank the men for their ideas and participation.

17. You are not expected to be a "perfect" leader. Just do the best you can by focusing on the partici-

pants and the lesson. God will help you lead this group. Enjoy your time together.

### ✦ Group Guidelines

Explain that this group is a family and that there are some ground rules for the benefit of the entire family. These rules include:

1. *Confidentiality.* What is said within the group stays within the group. Do not share personal information from this group with friends or your family. This is a safe place to talk.

2. *Purpose.* This is not a therapy group, a sensitivity group, or an encounter group. We are here to grow in faith and closer to God. We can offer Christian love and support to one another.

3. *Schedule.* Each session will start on time and end on time. Please be prompt. Let someone know if you are unable to attend.

4. *Equality.* All men in this group are equal. No one is expected to be an expert on a topic.

5. *Acceptance.* It is important that each man be accepted by the rest of the group just as he is. We are all members of God's family.

### ✦ Participant Guidelines

Read these guidelines to the group at the start of your first session:

1. What you will receive from this study will be in direct proportion to your involvement. Feel free to share your thoughts about the material being discussed. Participate as your comfort level permits.

2. Please be supportive of and encourage your fellow participants.

3. Please read the lesson and review the questions prior to the meeting. You may want to jot down answers to some of the questions.

4. You may be unable to answer some of the discussion questions. This is not a problem. No one has all the answers. Any ventured answer or guess is welcome.

5. There may be more than one answer to some questions.

6. Pray for your group and your leader.

Once you have reviewed the basics, you may or may not have time for discussion of the first lesson. If you have not done so already, you could distribute books and talk about the book. This is also a good time to solicit questions from your members. You could end the meeting with more social time or another icebreaker.

## ✧ Group Activities

Discussion questions can be followed by a group activity. An activity is an excellent way to encourage group interaction and the sharing of ideas and information. Activities can add depth to the topic being discussed. Here are some suggestions about planning an activity.

1. Some study guides include multiple suggestions for activities. This gives you the option of selecting which idea is best suited for your group. If you are not using a study guide, you or a group member can create your own activity. You'll want to set aside a specific amount of time for this event.

2. Select your activity in advance, and plan for it. If the activity requires pens and paper for the entire group, have them on hand. Drawing or creating something is a great group activity.

3. Your activity could be a group discussion on a specific topic. It may be creating a list of some sort related to your topic. If you come up with a hot question that lends itself to a lengthy discussion, use it in the activity section of your meeting.

4. Watching a movie or video as a group could be an activity. This could be followed by a group discussion.

5. After completing discussion questions, some groups use the Bible as a resource to delve into a specific aspect of a topic.

6. Magazines and newspapers often are used in an activity to search for local or national connections to a topic.

7. Try a field trip as an activity sometime over the course of your sessions. For example, if the topic is death or dying, a visit to a local cemetery or funeral home could be beneficial.

8. A practical application to what you are studying can become an excellent group activity. Visiting a nursing home as a group is a practical application for the topic of loneliness. Community service projects are also avenues to apply what you have been studying.

9. An activity could be a practical application after your meeting is over. It might be as simple as asking each member to share what he learned from this lesson with a family member or friend.

10. A challenge for the coming week could serve as an activity. For example, if the topic is kindness, the challenge could be to perform an act of kindness this week involving a total stranger. Members could report results at the next session.

# CHAPTER 4

# Sustaining Your Group

God cares for people through people. This is how your men's group will be sustained, as people minister to one another. As leader, you can't sustain and nurture your group alone. It is a group effort by you, your members, and God.

First, remember that your group is faith-based. Your faith and the faith of your members is how God works within your men's group. Prayer is one of the most important elements of sustaining a group. Your prayers, along with the prayers of your members, can work wonders in changing lives and drawing people closer to God. Prayer brings God in as an active participant in your men's group. Pray for your group and encourage members to do the same.

Second, remember the importance of being a good listener. Sometimes this involves listening to what is being said as well as to what is not. Listening can be just as vital to sustaining your group as words and actions. Listen for signs of men reaching out to other men for help. Keeping your ears open is an excellent way to keep an accurate sense of the members of your group. Remind your participants of the importance of being good listeners.

Third, encourage members to minister to each other. It can be as simple as phoning or emailing someone during the week to see how he is doing or having a cup of coffee with a member after the meeting ends. Sharing your faith with one member or the entire group is a wonderful ministry. It all comes down to showing you care and putting your faith into action. Again, your small group is not a therapy group, and members need to understand the difference. However, showing love and concern for others is what God wants us to do, and this will sustain your men's group.

Finally, remain receptive to God's Spirit. God does work in mysterious ways to bring healing and to change lives. Seeds may be planted in your group that will blossom years later. Your group will be sustained by God, and you simply have to trust in that. God brought you all together for a purpose. Let God's Spirit lead and sustain your ministry.

## ✧ Providing More Than You Promise

Sustaining your men's group is often a matter of being thoughtful and making that extra effort to minister to members of the group. The more you encourage your group to become a family, the healthier your group will be.

Creating a weekly or monthly newsletter about your group is one special touch that pays big dividends. It doesn't need to be anything fancy or elaborate. One side of a sheet of paper will do. You can include a list of upcoming events, a welcome to new members, personal news about members such as who just got a new job or a new car, birthday greetings, and any other information you deem appropriate. No postage is needed, as the newsletters can be handed out at meetings and posted on bulletin boards. Give a copy to the pastor and church council members to keep them informed.

Remembering and celebrating the birthdays of members as a group is a thoughtful touch. It can be as simple as singing "Happy Birthday" as a group or passing around a card to sign.

Encourage the deepening of friendships and networking by creating a master list of members' names and telephone numbers so men can keep in contact during the week. Get each man's permission before doing this. Include email addresses. Update and distribute monthly or as needed.

Helping one another creates "family" and "community" within your group. One opportunity to deepen relationships is to encourage members to be of service to one another. Helping a member move his belongings from one place to another can create bonding and is always appreciated.

### ✧ Growing Your Group

Sustaining your group means growing by welcoming new men each month. It's inevitable that some members of your group will move out of the area or drop out due to scheduling conflicts. How do you attract new men to your group?

The best way to attract new men to your group is to encourage your members to invite their friends to a meeting. Personal invitations get results because they reduce the anxiety in joining a new group. Men are less likely to show up if they do not know anyone. They are more likely to show up accompanied by a group member who can provide "security" and introduce the new guy to others.

The leader can also "grow the group" by maintaining and nurturing that initial list of prospective members who have not yet made it to a meeting. A telephone call or email to someone who was "busy" when the group was being formed may now find that person receptive. All it may take is a personal invitation from the leader or a member.

Leaders and members alike need to always be aware of how difficult it can be to walk into a room of people you do not know. Men who attend a meeting for the first time need to be welcomed and to feel welcome. You get one chance to make a first impression.

Follow-up is also important. When a new person attends, it is to your advantage to get his phone number so you can stay in contact. A few days after the meeting, phone him and see how things are going. All people are flattered that someone cares enough to remember them and call to talk.

Be aware that some first-timers will not be back. It may not be anything you or the group did. Perhaps they just didn't click with the group, or they didn't find what they were seeking. If you did your best in welcoming them, you have nothing to regret.

*A word of warning: Do not fall into the trap of judging the success of your group by the number of men who attend. A group of five men is just as valuable to God as a group of ten or twenty.*

## ✧ Solving Problems

There may be some bumps in the road on your journey. As in life, not everything goes the way you plan. You may need to adjust your original expectations and goals. God may be taking your group in another direction from the path you intended. So, what should you do if your group just does not seem to be working out?

First, figure out what is going on. Conducting an evaluation may help. If you make the effort to observe and listen to your group, you may be able to anticipate and head off many potential problems.

Second, if the problem is in your discussions, remember that the life span of a small group is a relatively brief time—six to eight weeks normally. Most small groups will not have the chance to gel much in such a short period of time. Do not expect the kind of group development you might look for in a group that has lived and shared together for years.

Third, keep in mind that although you are the leader, the main responsibility for how the group develops belongs to the group itself. You do the best you can to create a hospitable setting for your group's interactions. You do your homework to keep the discussion and interactions flowing. But ultimately, every member of the group individually and corporately bears responsibility for whatever happens within the life of the small group.

However, if any specific problems do show up, try these suggestions:

**If new people feel uncomfortable or unwelcome**, the problem and solution belong to your entire group. Established groups that are ongoing without any ending date may get too comfortable with the "regulars" and develop into cliques. This is normal. The problem starts when a new person shows up and feels like an outsider.

First, it is normal for a new person to feel like an outsider. They don't know anyone. New people are obligated to make an extra effort to become part of the group. Second, your group members need to be reminded to be sensitive to the needs of new people.

"Regulars" need to go out of their way to talk to and include new people. As a leader, you can be a role model by being the first to welcome new people and by introducing them to each member of the group.

**If one member dominates the group** or small-group discussions, help the group identify this problem for itself by asking group members to rate overall participation. In other words, get a discussion going about how your discussions and activities are going. Another option is to ask a discussion question with the request that each person respond briefly. As a leader, you can practice gatekeeping during group discussions by saying, "We've heard from Joe; now what does someone else think?" If the problem continues, speak gently outside of a group session with the member who dominates.

**If one member is reluctant to participate** in a discussion, ask each member to respond briefly to a discussion question in a round-robin fashion. Another option is to ask a reluctant participant what he thinks of a topic or question. You can also increase participation by dividing the larger group into smaller groups of two or three men.

**If your group strays from the topic** during a discussion, judge whether the group has a legitimate reason for straying. By straying from your agenda, is the group setting an agenda more valid for their needs? Another option simply is to restate the original topic or question. If one individual keeps causing the group to inappropriately stray from the topic, speak to him outside of a session.

**If someone drops out of the group,** it might be because his needs are not being met within the group. You will never know unless you ask that person directly. You should contact a person immediately following a first unplanned absence. Otherwise, they are unlikely to return.

**If someone shares a big, dangerous, or bizarre problem,** remember that your men's group is not a therapy group. You should not take on the responsibility of "fixing" someone else's problem. You should encourage a member who shares a major problem to seek professional help. If necessary, remind the group about the need for confidentiality. If someone shares something that endangers either himself or someone else, contact your pastor for advice.

### ✧ Evaluating

How do you know if your men's group is healthy? In order to sustain your group, some regular evaluation is smart. As a leader, your observations, which can be based on your feelings, are important. You should also evaluate with input from participants. You may want to evaluate your group after several meetings rather than waiting until the end. Here are some ideas on how to evaluate your group:

Find out whether the group is measuring up to what the members expected of it. Go back to your first meeting where members said why they came to the meeting. Ask members how well this experience measures up to their expectations.

Ask how members perceive group dynamics. Using a scale from one to ten, with ten being the highest, ask them to rate the overall participation by members of the group. On the same scale, where would they rate this group as meeting their needs? On the same scale, how would they rate the "togetherness" of this men's group?

Ask group members to fill out an evaluation sheet. Keep the evaluation form simple. One of the simplest forms leaves plenty of blank space for responding to three requests: (1) Name the three things you want to do more of. (2) Name the three things you want to do less of. (3) Name the three things you want to keep the same.

Ask for direct feedback from one participant. Arrange ahead of time for a group member to stay a few minutes after a meeting or to meet with you the next day. Ask for direct feedback about what seemed to work or not work, who seems to be participating well, who seems to be dealing with something particularly troubling, and so forth.

Give group members permission to say when they sense something is not working. As the group leader, you do not hold responsibility for the life of the group. The group's life belongs to all the members. Encourage members to take responsibility for what takes place within the group setting.

Expect and accept that, at times, discussions will fall flat, group interaction will be stilted, and group members will be grumpy. All groups have bad days. Moreover, all groups go through their own life cycles. Although your new group may take time to gel completely, you may find that after two or three sessions, one session will come when nothing seems to go right. That is normal. In fact, studies show that those groups that first show a little conflict eventually begin to move into deeper levels of relationships.

Sit back and observe. In the middle of a group discussion, sit back and try to look at the group as a whole. Does it look healthy to you? Is one person dominating? Does someone else seem to be withdrawn? How would you best describe what you observe going on within the group?

Take the "temperature" of the group. Try asking the group to take its own temperature. Would it be normal? below-normal? feverish? What adjective would you use to describe the group's temperature?

Keep a record of evaluations. Use some form of evaluation several times during the life of the group. Compare them and see how your group has changed.

## ✧ Making Changes

In order to sustain your men's group, some changes may be in order. These changes may be large or small, depending on the needs of the group. You should consult the group before making any changes. Solicit their opinions and ideas.

Changing the time or day of the meeting is commonly necessary. If attendance is a problem, a better time period or new day could help. You may need to meet at a different time in order to accommodate the needs of one or more people. Discuss this with all group members before coming to a decision.

Over time, leadership may need to change. In this situation, the current leader should be honest with the group. Give the group some notice and time to adjust. A new leader could be selected through a volunteer process or handpicked by the current leader. It is helpful if the new leader can be given some training or support from the old leader.

## ✧ Calling It Quits

There is a beginning and end to everything, including a men's group. In some cases, your group experience may have a preplanned ending at the conclusion of an eight- or twelve-week discussion. If so, the end will come as no surprise to the participants. Some will be ready to move on. Others may be disappointed and have trouble letting go. Here are some suggestions on how to conclude your meetings:

If you are concluding your small-group discussion or a Bible study, end the final discussion with some open-ended questions designed for closure. *What was your favorite chapter, and why? What did you learn about yourself and others from studying this book? How has participation in this men's group changed you?* Plan for a longer-than-normal discussion time. Close with a prayer giving thanks for the group and the participants.

Plan a brief social time at the conclusion of the final session. Give participants a chance to mingle, chat, and say their farewells. Have some soft drinks and snacks available. If all of the participants approve, create a list of names, phone numbers, and email addresses so participants can keep in touch. Thank the group members for their participation and for ministering to one another. Offer any observations you feel appropriate about the growth of the group and individuals.